Beauty
from
My Ashes

Beauty
from
My Ashes

Gloria Anderson

1603 Capitol Ave., Suite 310 Cheyenne, Wyoming USA 82001
1-888-980-6523 | admin@urlinkpublishing.com

URLink Print and Media is committed to excellence in the publishing industry.

Published in the United States of America

ISBN 978-1-68486-381-5 (Paperback)
ISBN 978-1-68486-383-9 (Hardback)
ISBN 978-1-68486-384-6 (Digital)

23.02.23

INTO CAPTIVITY

The clock on the wall ticks in half-time to my racing heart. Though others are in the waiting room with me, none of our eyes meet. The receptionist ignores all of us and goes on about her business. A heavy fog of shame, fear, and regret covers me, weighing me down, causing me to sink even lower in the seat and in my own self-image. My mother and sister sit silently beside me, each lost in their own thoughts about why we are here. I am afraid to look at my mother – afraid to see the shame and disappointment I believe will be there. I had let down the most important person in my life. Though I desperately want and need to climb up into her lap like I did when I was a small child to cling to her and have her make everything all right, I know I can't. Not this time. She can't make this better. She can't make this go away. I sink lower in the seat, thinking back to how I ended up here . . .

Chapter One

A Wounded Childhood

Hot, lazy summer days. My brothers, neighbors and I playing in cold running creeks. The smell of honeysuckle and locust in the air so thick I can almost taste it. Mosquito bites and honeybee stings. The sounds of birds chirping, singing and squawking, making life seem light and happy. The sound of laughter filling the air as we cool off under the spray of a well-treasured garden hose. Mud pies consisting of the greatest concoctions imagined by a child. Playing Red Rover, One-Two-Three Red Light, Mother-May-I, hopscotch and jacks for hours on end. Going outside in the early morning and embarking on great adventures and fun-loving games until hunger or Mom called us in. Family gatherings that included lots of laughter, fun, teasing and great food. Mother singing, Dad joking, brothers teasing, sisters teaching. Lots of laughter, lots of fun, lots of hugs, lots of . . . . . love.

I have many such memories of my childhood, long-forgotten amidst the years of darkness that invaded and eventually overshadowed the sense of who I was and where I came from. Memories that struggled to breathe through the fog of betrayal, pain, shame and despair that permeated the innocence that was my childhood; memories choked almost to extinction, growing weaker with each passing year until innocence was gone and knowledge of things best left unknown by a child became the memories that dominated my mind.

I was the sixth and final child born to a wonderful hard-working, God-loving couple. Though we didn't go to church much, they taught us about God's love for us by sending His Son, Jesus, to die for our sins. I have enjoyable memories of going to Vacation Bible School, making crafts and learning about Jesus. My Mom and Dad treated all people the same, regardless of their color, their money (or lack thereof) or what they did for a living. When you came to our house, you were family.

My parents loved each other and loved their children, and did the best they could to provide for each of us. Though we didn't have a lot, we were taught to take good care of what we did have and to be appreciative of it. We were expected to eat what was cooked and couldn't leave the table before we did. It didn't take me long to learn that warm brussel sprouts tasted better than cold ones!

My mother was a kind, gentle, loving, affectionate, quiet, dependable and loyal woman. She not only worked a full-time job, but she also took care of her family. My father was a strong, loving, affectionate, funny, laughing and boisterous man. Unfortunately, he was also an alcoholic and he came from a family of alcoholics. When he drank, he could become a completely different kind of man - angry, yelling, and . . . . scary. I never saw him hit my mother, but I did see him be rough with her and I did hear him yell horrible insulting and degrading things at her. This was so opposite of the father I usually saw and it filled my mind with confusion and my heart with fear. I became afraid of someone that I should have been able to trust completely. The first impressions of my value as a female began to form in my heart.

Gatherings in our family always included food and drinking, and much of both. Fortunately, my mother drank very little, if any, so I always had her to turn to when things got crazy. These gatherings always made me nervous because I never knew when things were going to change from fun to fear, from happy to angry, from playing to fighting. Many angry and violent incidents occurred in our family because of too much alcohol.

When I was around the age of five, we were having a gathering and a family friend was sitting and drinking by himself behind the house in the back yard. I had been playing in the side yard and chased a ball or toy into the back yard. The family friend motioned for me to come over and I happily complied, thinking in my childish innocence that he had something to give me. He told me to give him a hug - which was a normal and customary request in our family - and I gladly responded. However, as I started to move out of his embrace, his hold tightened and his hand began to touch me in places that had never been touched by a man before. Surprise, shock, confusion and fear flooded my tender young mind. It didn't occur to me to scream or yell; it didn't occur to me to hit him or try to wrench away. I trusted him and though I felt he was doing something wrong to me, it didn't hurt so I didn't know WHAT to do. He whispered quiet words of assurance to me just to stay there and told me what a good little girl I was. I don't know if he heard something or realized we were in plain view, but he suddenly let me go. He thanked me and asked me if that had hurt. I shook my head. He asked me if it had felt good. I nodded my head. He told me not to tell anyone or we would both get into a lot of trouble. The first tendrils of shame began to weave their way into my soul like ivy beginning to grow up the side of a wall, and another impression of my value as a female was formed in my heart.

Encounters with this family friend happened several times over the course of my childhood. He would beckon me over with a smile and ask for a hug. He would touch me for a few minutes, then thank me, tell me what a good little girl I was, and send me back off to play. He would give me a piece of candy and a soft warning not to tell anyone or we would be in trouble. Every time it happened, I both dreaded it and enjoyed it . . . . and I told no one.

Over the next five or six years, I had similar experiences with other family friends and relatives. Sometimes the touching hurt and sometimes it felt good, but it always made me feel ashamed and fearful of getting caught. These men would whisper words of affirmation of what a good girl I was and how good touching me and my touching them made them feel. Afterwards, they would warn me not to say anything and send me on my way. Each time, the conflicting emotions of repulsion and enjoyment I felt filled my young mind with confusion, fear and guilt. I lived my young life carrying around a very big, shameful secret. If I resisted, threats of all the damage and trouble I would cause were given, subtly telling me what was happening was MY fault. The dark fingers of shame crept even deeper into my being, like a thick fog on a cold, rainy night. I was also beginning to learn the lie that letting a man touch me for his pleasure made me valuable to him. This lie would come to shape my choices and my self-image for years to come . . . . and I told no one.

A solemn-faced nurse comes to the door and calls my name. My mind screams to run out the front door and never stop running, but instead my feet take me toward the nurse and toward what I know to be wrong, but don't know how to stop. I am 15 and almost 12 weeks pregnant. And I am terrified. Terrified to go through with this abortion and terrified to not go through with it. The voice that I've heard nonstop for the past week continues to speak in my head . . . "You're too young to be a mother. You can't take care of a baby. You have a life ahead of you. You can't give a baby any kind of life. You are going to college to be a nurse. You'll have to give that all up to raise a child. Your boyfriend is 19! Your dad will put him in jail for getting you pregnant. Can you live with that? Your boyfriend didn't ask to be a daddy. You won't be a good mother. Your baby won't have a good life. You're doing the best thing for this baby. It's the right decision. It's the only decision . . ."

Chapter Two

Misplaced Self-Worth

During the year of my 11th birthday, we moved to a new neighborhood and the molesting stopped. Unfortunately, by that time I had come to believe that my value and likability were dependent upon whether or not people were pleased with me. Even though both my parents loved me unconditionally and always expressed their love toward me, because I had been betrayed by other friends and relatives who I should have been able to trust, I had developed a deep insecurity about someone's true feelings towards me. I didn't feel I was likable and felt I had to EARN someone's affection. I was filled with such a deep sense of shame and self-disgust for the things I thought I had allowed to happen that I could not allow myself to believe I was worthy of love. These feelings were reinforced when I tried to make friends in our new neighborhood.

Exploring the neighborhood, it wasn't long before I noticed a group of girls that seemed to represent everything I wanted to be – pretty, nicely dressed and feminine. Excited, I approached them and attempted to befriend them. Unfortunately, they were not very friendly and I did not feel welcome. The pain of their rejection pierced deep into my soul, further affirming my opinion that I was unlikeable.

Lonely and desperate for friendship, I soon reached out to another group of girls in the neighborhood, the girls that looked more like me and dressed in worn jeans or shorts and battered tennis shoes. They had an air of toughness that appealed to me. Growing up with mostly only boys to play with, my usual outside attire consisted of clothes that could handle rough play and getting dirty, so I felt these were my kind of girls. I approached them with all the confidence I could muster and to my delight I was welcomed warmly. Finally! I had friends! Finally! I had girls to play with! Relief washed over me that day like a downpour of cool rain on a hot, humid summer's day. I believed I no longer had to live being afraid or lonely. Life was good.

Playing with my brothers and their friends in my previous neighborhood, I had learned to play rough and tough. I enjoyed climbing trees, playing football, rough-housing, basketball, wrestling, etc. As I became better acquainted with the kids in my new neighborhood, I was eventually asked to play in the various games that were going on, which included football in undeveloped lots or nearby fields. The boys soon learned that I was a very good football player "for a girl," and I was tougher than most. I knew both how to dodge a tackle and to make one. I could take down a guy much bigger than me, though I really enjoyed the rare chances to tackle one of the girls. I also had good hands when it came to catching the football. While the boys on the opposing team scrambled to cover the guys on my team, I was only covered by other girls who were no match for my abilities. They mostly just giggled sheepishly, acted completely helpless and brainless, and ran from the ball when it was thrown to them, squealing in fright. As a result, I scored many touchdowns for my team, making me a valuable asset. It wasn't long before I became one of the first girls picked for a team. This made me feel important, needed and wanted; qualities that I had not previously considered described me.

Unfortunately, while being wanted by the guys on the teams made me feel proud of myself, some of the other girls didn't particularly like it. Unlike me, they didn't understand that when it came to sports guys were always serious about wanting to win. They also didn't understand that the boys did not see me as one of the "pretty" girls. The boys just wanted to win the game and these girls just didn't know the first thing about playing football. Sometimes some of the girls would make derogatory comments that hurt my feelings or rude comments meant to embarrass me. I struggled to hold on to the budding self-esteem my recent popularity had started to nurture. Statements such as, "They only want you on their team because you play like a boy! They don't really like you." found their intended mark. It was only WHAT I DID that mattered to people, not WHO I WAS.

At the ripe old age of 11, I believed my lack of value had already been determined and there was nothing I could do to change it. I believed that I was WORTHLESS. This would shape my attitude and direct my choices for years to come.

BECOMING A PRISONER

I follow the nurse down a long hall and into a room on the right. There is a table in the middle that seems way too big for the room. I am told to take off my clothes and put on this gown. The nurse never smiles. She doesn't even bother to look at me. The heavy fog of shame lowers once again over me. I am dirt. I am a slut. I am an evil person. I have let everyone down. I am a failure. The door closes. I start undressing . . .

Chapter Three

Self-Destruction

Having succumbed to the lie that I was worthless, and desperate for the approval of my friends, it wasn't long before I was doing what they were doing and even inventing mischief and rebellion myself for others to join in with me. Mentally, however, I felt like a rabbit chasing a carrot that was dangling just out of my reach; constantly trying to obtain something that was impossible to obtain, yet unable to stop trying to obtain it. Emotionally, I once again felt fear - fear of rejection, fear of getting caught doing the things I was doing and fear of my parents' disappointment if I did get caught. Both my parents worked full-time jobs and they got home almost exactly at 5:25 every evening. I got home from school about 3:15 every day. I learned to make the most of that 2 hours and 10 minutes.

At the tender age of 12, I started smoking cigarettes and marijuana. At school, I recruited a small group of 3 girls and a guy that I would try to convince to go along with my rebellious schemes. We would sneak cigarettes and marijuana joints into school and try to find opportunities to smoke them. Though I was never disrespectful to my teachers verbally, I resisted their authority in other ways, mostly by talking or purposely not paying attention. Back then kids got paddled for misbehavior. It soon became a source of pride for me to see how many times I got paddled and how many "licks" I could stand. The barest hint of respect, admiration or fear from my peers fueled my behavior like a spark to a gasoline-soaked rag. I was living the saying, "Bad attention is better than no attention." Teachers noticed me, fellow students noticed me. Terrified of walking through life invisible, I grasped onto anything that made someone acknowledge that I was alive.

Smoking cigarettes and marijuana with my friends began to consume the time I used to spend at home with my parents. Marijuana temporarily made me feel happy and pushed away the almost constant feelings of fear and shame, while at the same time breeding its own brand of fear and shame. Though I had always enjoyed spending time with my parents, talking to my mother and watching TV with my father became more a chore rather than a pleasure. All my focus was on being with my friends, getting high, and being accepted.

It wasn't long, however, before the cigarettes and marijuana were not enough. One of us came up with the idea of "huffing", which involved taking a can of Pam cooking spray and inhaling the fumes through a rag. This would cause us to pass out for a few seconds and wake with a tingling, humming sound and a feeling of euphoria. Of course, we had no idea that we were playing Russian Roulette with our brains - that one whiff could kill us or make us brain dead. All we cared about was how it made us feel.

At the age of 13, I began drinking alcohol and taking pills along with the marijuana. Though I had grown up in a somewhat alcohol-induced violent atmosphere, I began enjoying how alcohol made me feel. It seemed I was not as shy and I felt more self-confident. I gradually learned how much to drink to keep those feelings without the vomiting that I detested. I also liked the feeling I got with the various pills my friends gave me. For that brief period of time, I was not afraid or worried and I could pretend that I was beautiful, popular and accepted.

My friends and I began sneaking out in the middle of the night. The sense of freedom was exhilarating and the danger of getting caught added to the excitement. One night, coming back home after running the neighborhood in the wee hours of the night, my mother was waiting at the door for me. She was furious; I had never seen my normally passive and cheerful mother so angry. She gave me a well-deserved slap across the face and sent me to my room. I never snuck out at night again.

Some of the friends I was running around with were older and already sexually active. Because of the events in my early childhood I had no interest in sex, but I did envy the affection I witnessed between my friends and their boyfriends. I yearned to have a guy look at me the way those guys seemingly looked at my friends. But I was such a tomboy - foul-mouthed, crass and mostly dressed to hide my shape – that most of those guys did not even notice I existed.

Then one day, still at the age of 12, I met Eric (name changed to protect privacy). Eric was the cutest boy I had seen up until then. He had blonde hair and gorgeous blue eyes. He was kind, polite and funny. He was quick to laugh and had a beautiful smile. The most amazing thing to me about Eric was that he actually seemed to like me. He always treated me with respect while at the same time letting me know that he was very attracted to me. While Eric dabbled with a little drinking and getting high with me, he basically was a good guy with a good head on his shoulders.

Looking back, I think I just didn't feel myself worthy of someone as good as Eric and perhaps believed it was only a matter of time before he would dump me for someone prettier, smarter, more lady-like or just more . . . valuable. While still hanging out with Eric, I met an older boy named Martin (named changed to protect privacy). I was surprised that he seemed interested in me and was very hesitant to trust his attention. Months went by and Martin continued to come around and shower me with attention. I couldn't believe an older boy actually liked me!!! The feeling was incredible; maybe I WAS pretty; maybe I WAS somebody to be noticed.

I found myself thinking about Martin more and Eric less and it wasn't long before I ended my relationship with Eric and poured all my attention and affection on Martin. As any 13 year old girl does, I dreamed of Martin and I married with children living in a little house with a picket fence. As Martin's kisses grew more passionate and his hands more demanding, I ignored the warnings going off in my mind, telling myself it was different with Martin. He was different. He really loved me and we were going to be together forever . . .

Martin's demands for sex began subtly enough, camouflaged within affirmations of his love for me, how beautiful I was, and how much he wanted us to express our love for each other in the most beautiful way possible. He then began making little statements hinting that he might have to start looking somewhere else if I didn't love him enough to express my love with my body. The old feelings of insecurity and not being enough for someone resurfaced, followed closely by the familiar sick, ugly fear and dread that I had thought long gone. My 13-year-old heart loved Martin and I realized that I wasn't enough; that if I wanted to keep him I would have to give him the one thing he wanted . . . my virginity.

Most young girls dream of their wedding night – the night they lose their virginity – as some romantic, beautiful, incredible experience. I was no different – except for the fact that I had started having those dreams at a much younger age than most girls. Unfortunately, at that same young age of 13, I made the choice to forfeit my right to that experience in the desperate hope of keeping the affections of a 19-year-old guy I thought I could not live without. My dream was shattered in the back seat of a car on a mountain dirt road while other cars passed by. It was a miserable, painful and disappointing experience. There were no words of love from this man I thought loved me. There was no tenderness or kindness. There was only his raw need and his determination to satisfy that need.

I had heard from my friends that sex was a wonderful thing. On TV, it looked so romantic and enjoyable. What I experienced wasn't wonderful, romantic OR enjoyable. It was painful and Martin showed no compassion or understanding of my feelings whatsoever. Immediately afterwards, as I sought comfort, affection and reassurance of his love for me, I instead heard the words that caused my heart to turn cold and feel like it was literally breaking apart: "You made me feel so good." I felt vomit rise to the back of my throat and I realized I had made a terrible, irreversible mistake. He dropped me off and I walked home with my head down, reeling from the choice I had made and feeling dirty, ashamed, unwanted, and rejected. Familiar feelings . . . hated feelings . . . what had I done?

From then on, my relationship with Martin revolved around finding a place where he could have sex with me. There was no longer any flirting. We didn't play games or spend time talking. It was just about the sex, and soon afterwards he would take me back home. He didn't care where we had sex and I didn't try to stop him. Sometimes it was out in the open. Sometimes it was in dirty, filthy abandoned houses or trailers. Sometimes it was on a dirty floor or outside on the ground. Sometimes it was on a nasty bed.

Though I hated each and every occasion, it was the only time I got the attention and affection from him that I used to get from him all the time before we started having sex. For those few short moments, I could pretend he loved me and thought I was beautiful, rather than just a means for his physical satisfaction. The act itself was not pleasant for me at all and I learned to kind of separate myself from what was happening and focus instead on making it end as quickly as possible.

I do not remember how long our relationship lasted. Eventually Martin moved on to someone else and I was left with the knowledge that I had given my most precious gift to someone who really didn't care about me. I felt humiliated, embarrassed and betrayed . . . and it was entirely my own fault.

My experience with Martin gave birth to another lie that fed off the previous one from my early childhood. I believed that if I wanted a boy to like me and want me for a girlfriend, then I had to have sex with him, and I foolishly decided to quit fighting what seemed inevitable. From the age of 13 through 15, there were many boys and some men. Some lasted days. Some lasted weeks. Some lasted months. Some were my age, some older, some much older. Some were even married.

Because I craved the feeling of being loved and wanted, even if just for a few moments, I accepted whatever situation I found myself in. Whether it was degrading, embarrassing, painful or shameful, I allowed my body to be used solely for the guy's pleasure. Though I never enjoyed it, I couldn't risk the rejection I was sure I'd receive if I refused so I just focused on getting it over as quickly as possible. This, however, only added to my feelings of shame and self-loathing. I was caught in a humiliating, self-destructive cycle that I didn't know how to stop.

By the age of 15, I was living a double life. I had learned to hide what was happening from my parents. They had no clue of the dark life their daughter lived while they were at work and when they thought I was at a friend's house. I hated my life. I hated being me. The lure of drugs and alcohol to dull the pain and self-disgust that threatened to eat me alive became stronger and harder to resist. I would take handfuls of different kinds of pills, chasing them down with wine or whiskey, with absolutely no thought to the danger of what I was doing. Believing my life had no value, I thought nothing about doing things that could end it. I got into cars with strange men, took all kinds of pills with alcohol, huffed nitrous oxide for hours, had sex with whoever seemed to take a liking to me and put myself in situations where I could be raped or murdered – in fact, being raped on one occasion – all the while pretending to my family and everyone else that I was happy and doing just fine. Sometimes the pain of yet another broken heart or the shame from another degrading event or the humiliation from another stupid decision would seem like more than I could bear; the emotions so thick and raw and . . . consuming that I just wanted it to end. I wanted ME to end. Though the desire to die was there, a plan never formed in my mind. It remained just an ever-present, sometimes contemplated desire that would lie dormant for years. One day, however, that desire would roar to life, demanding consideration and becoming the catalyst for one of the greatest changes in my life.

The nurse comes back in and helps me onto the table. The doctor comes in, and with a stern, disapproving face and voice asks me did I not realize that having sex could get me pregnant? The fog of shame gets thicker. The nurse puts my feet in stirrups. I want to scream and run out of there, but I know I can't. No baby deserves me for a mother. My parents deserve better than me for a daughter. The nurse stretches out my arm and begins inserting the IV . . .

Chapter Four

A Panicked Decision

By the age of 15, I had finally come to realize that I could get pregnant so I decided that no matter what I was not going to have sex with my next boyfriend. During the fall of my 15th year, I was reacquainted with an older boy named Jake (name changed to protect privacy) whom I had known as a friend of my brothers. He showed an interest in dating me and I was thrilled. He was even interested in asking my parents' permission to take me out. Unknown to me at the time, Jake had heard about my sexual encounter with another older guy who had previously given me a ride and required me to have sex with him before he would take me home. Presumably, Jake believed I was an "easy" girl to have sex with.

Surprisingly, my parents agreed; probably because they had known him for so many years. I was so excited about having an older boyfriend! Wouldn't all the pretty girls be jealous? And he seemed to really be interested in ME. Disappointingly, we only went out on a few dates before his interest in me changed and he started pressuring me to have sex with him. One particular night, Jake was being very persistent in his quest to have sex with me and I was enjoying all the affection and passion. However, in my strongest, most confident voice, I informed him that I would not have sex with him because I didn't want to get pregnant. I remember thinking, *"There! I said it! Now we can just get back to dating.*

Wait a minute! What did he just say? He was injured playing high school football and was told he can't be a father so we don't have to worry about me getting pregnant? Now, what do I do?" Feeling helpless, I give in yet again to what I despise, but feel I have no power to prevent and no right to refuse. The pattern I've come to know only too well falls into place with Jake as it had with all the others. Every date has only one purpose and I resign myself to the inevitable.

The first knot of fear welled up in my throat. I felt like I was going to vomit. My period hadn't come. I thought to myself, *"I can't be pregnant! Jake said he couldn't be a father. It must just be some quirk with my body. There's no way I'm pregnant."* I chose to ignore it, hoping against hope that my period would come the next month. The knot of fear persisted, though I kept pushing it to the back of my mind. The next month came and still no period. By that time, the knot had become a gigantic fist of terror in the pit of my stomach. I confided in a friend and she suggested I go to the health department for a pregnancy test. I forged my mother's signature on the form and gave a urine sample. My friend and I sat in the waiting room. I cried out to a God that I never talked to, listened to or cared much about except when I was in trouble. *"Please God, don't let me be pregnant. I'll be a good girl, I promise. I've learned my lesson. No more sex for me! I won't have sex again until I'm married if you'll just not let me be pregnant."* I heard my name called. I went back into the nurse's office . . .

I was approximately 11 weeks pregnant. My mind went blank and then thoughts began racing through my mind, *"Pregnant! I'm pregnant? This can't be happening! What am I going to tell my parents? My parents! They are going to kill me! My dad will have my boyfriend put in jail. They are going to be so disappointed in me! I can't be a mother! I'm too young to be a mother!"* In a matter-of-fact voice, the nurse informed me that I must have an abortion that week or I would have to be hospitalized for the procedure because the law required any abortion past 12 weeks be done in a hospital. She gave me the name of the local abortion clinic. She offered no other options or counsel. I walked out feeling numb and emotionless, yet at the same time filled with all sorts of emotions. Fear and shame mixed with something akin to excitement. I touched my belly. A baby. I've got a baby inside me. *How am I going to tell my mother? What do I say?*

I told my oldest sister who took me to tell my mother. I will never forget the look on my mother's face. It haunted me for years. She knew before I told her. She hugged me and told me she loved me, but I could feel the hurt in her body and hear it in her voice. *I failed you, Mom. I'm so sorry! I'm so sorry! I wish I could go back and change things.* Possibly trying to make a bad situation seemingly better, I told her that there was a place that would do an abortion quickly so that Dad would never have to know.

I think I was relieved that a way existed to make this gigantic problem go away. I had been thinking about the reality of being pregnant and I didn't like what it meant. I would have to drop out of school. I had plans to go to college. My father would know I had been having sex. My boyfriend was 19 and he would have him arrested for statutory rape. The kids at school would know I had been having sex and was stupid enough to get pregnant.

Since time was of the essence, they scheduled the abortion for two days later. Soon, it would just be a forgotten memory of a bad mistake . . .

I can feel the drug working its way up my arm, into my shoulder and up my neck. The sweetest, warmest feeling comes over me. I feel completely relaxed. I hear something loud. To my drug-dulled mind it sounds like a vacuum cleaner. What's a vacuum cleaner doing in the room? Wait a minute! That's not a vacuum cleaner! It's coming from where the doctor is. What's he going to do with it? I feel something being inserted inside me. It's cold. He's putting the vacuum inside me. Oh, so that's how it's done. I expect to hear one loud suck and then it's over. But no, I hear another sound . . . a terrible sound . . . it reminds me of when I'm at the bottom of a very thick shake and I'm trying to suck the last little bits up the straw. Hold on! Why IS it making that sound? There's only one baby, right? Then why does it sound like little pieces of milkshake being sucked up through the straw? What . . .?

Chapter Five

Loss of Identity

I have no memory of the end of the abortion or leaving the abortion clinic. My first memory is being in the car heading to my sister-in-law's to recuperate. The voice I'd heard since I found out I was pregnant now began to speak again, but this time the tone was menacing, accusing, hateful. *"You've just killed your own baby! What kind of monster does that? What kind of person are you? How could you do that to your own child? You're a murderer! A baby-killer! No man will ever want you now. God will never forgive you for this! Never! How could you do that?* I believed that voice and I lived the next 20 or more years under the identity that voice described.

I had to go to school the next day following my abortion and pretend like nothing had happened, though the blood I could see every time I went to the bathroom reminded me that something had, in fact happened. Something horrible. Something violent. From the day of my abortion, the feelings of worthlessness, low-esteem and self-loathing intensified. I just simply hated myself and saw no reason at all for my existence. For the next week or so, the tell-tale bleeding was a constant reminder of the violence that I had allowed to take place in my womb; that a baby who once lived there no longer existed. As the months went by, I imagined what my belly would have looked like. When I saw pregnant women looking so happy, I was filled with such intense shame and regret that it was unbearable. My baby's due date would have been around my 16th birthday. Though I tried my best not to remember, not to think about it, my child had already imprinted itself on my heart. Yet, I could not grieve; I had no right. I could not share my heartache with anyone; I had chosen the abortion. I dared not speak to God about it. How could I? I had done the single most horrible thing a person could do! You can't share that stuff with God! I believed the voice that said God would never forgive me and I felt I had no right to ask Him to. In order to survive, I had to learn to live with what I had done and forget about it.

As the years went by, I did learn how to hide those feelings. I learned to laugh on the outside while I was crying on the inside, much like I had done the majority of my life. The defense mechanisms I had developed as a child when I was being molested came in handy in separating myself from what I had done. I learned to appear confident when I was really terrified. I learned to be outgoing even though I felt very shy. When the abortion controversy became very public, I took the side of the "pro-choice" movement and tried to tell myself I was justified in what I had done. My life came before my baby's. I was more important than a child. Maybe it wasn't even a baby to begin with.

My boyfriend and I continued dating and being sexually active (though with use of birth control). He broke up with me shortly after that because he said I was different, and I was. I was a young girl who had killed her baby and had no one to talk to about it. There was one friend I had who had had 3 abortions, but she didn't want to talk about it and said it wasn't a big deal to her. Therefore, it was a secret shame that I had to keep to myself and deal with by myself. I never spoke about my abortion. My family never spoke about it. My father never knew.

Over the years, my self-destructive behavior only intensified. I did harder drugs and drank more. Many times I wished I would just never wake up. There was no good in me. I had nothing to offer anyone except my body and many times even that seemed to not be enough in the long run. I honestly didn't understand why God didn't just go ahead and kill me.

Isaiah 61:1-3

1 *"The Spirit of the Lord GOD is upon Me,*
Because the LORD has anointed Me to
preach good tidings to the poor;
He has sent Me to heal the brokenhearted,
to proclaim liberty to the captives,
And the opening of the prison to those who are bound;
2 *to proclaim the acceptable year of the LORD,*
and the day of vengeance of our God;
to comfort all who mourn,
3 *to console those who mourn in Zion,*
to give them beauty for ashes,
the oil of joy for mourning,
the garment of praise for the spirit of despair;
That they may be called trees of righteousness,
Planted by the LORD, that He may be glorified."

Chapter Six

An Act of Desperation

*"The Spirit of the Lord GOD is upon Me,
because the LORD has anointed Me . . ."*

I got married soon after graduating high school and a few years later had two wonderful children. Unfortunately, I had no confidence in myself as a woman, a wife or a mother and I increasingly began to doubt my ability to parent my children. Sometimes I felt like such a complete failure in everything. I hated myself so much. I became divorced after 10 years of marriage and had to learn to face life as single mother. This only increased my self-doubt and insecurities. I did not trust my judgment where men were concerned and I was terrified I would bring some sort of pedophiliac monster into my children's lives. Driven by fear, I remember asking God to please bring a man who would be a good father to my children. I didn't feel worthy enough to ask for a man who would be good to me, but I did not want my children to suffer because their mother was such a failure in life.

God did in fact bring such a man into our lives and after three years of getting to know one another, we got married in one of the little chapels in Pigeon Forge, TN. The children were thrilled, my husband was thrilled . . . and I was grateful that someone so wonderful not only loved my children, but seemed to love me as well. Unfortunately, my insecurities still plagued me and caused many unnecessary quarrels between us. There were many times I was certain he was going to walk out the door and never return - and I wouldn't have blamed him - but he never did.

About six years later, there came a point in my life when I believed the only solution I could see to end everyone's misery for having to deal with me was to kill myself. I developed a plan and began gearing myself up for the courage to go through with it. As the time approached, however, a thought kept coming to my mind; one that reminded me how much I loved my children, how much they loved me and how much it would hurt them if I died. In a weird way, this only added to my guilt and shame. I then had the thought of would I go to heaven if I killed myself? I didn't know the answer. I wasn't sure if I had done what I needed to in order to go to heaven. I remembered as a young child going to Vacation Bible School and hearing about what a terrible place hell was and I asked Jesus to save me, but I wasn't sure if that really took since I had hardly thought of Him except in times of trouble. I then started thinking that if I killed myself and I hadn't done what was necessary to go to heaven, then I wouldn't be able to come back and change my mind and I would go to hell. That absolutely terrified me. Yet, how could a woman who had killed her child and done all sorts of other sinful things go to heaven? How could God forgive someone like me? Again, I didn't know the answer, but it was enough to stop me from going through with my suicide plan. I decided to continue on with life just to be safe, never telling anyone how close I had come to ending it, but I knew something in my life had to change.

I don't remember why exactly, but soon after my choice to keep living there came a point in time when I started feeling drawn to the local church my teenage children attended. I had met several members of that church and they had always been nice and friendly. One particular Sunday, I decided I would go; not exactly sure what I was hoping to find, but knowing deep inside that I had to go.

I entered the church and discovered that a revival service was going on and a visiting preacher was speaking. I don't remember the message. I don't remember any specific thing that was said. What I do remember is understanding deep down inside that I had come to talk to Jesus, and He was waiting for me. Silently, unaware of my surroundings, I poured out my heart to the God I had ignored for so many years, who I had blamed for the bad things in my life, who I had believed was a mean, easily angered God who expected us to be perfect, yet who I had also been told loved us. While I don't remember exactly what I said to Him, it went something like this . . . *"Jesus, I can't go on like this anymore. I hate myself! I absolutely hate myself! There's nothing I like about me. I'm a failure at everything! I'm a failure as a mother. I'm a terrible wife. I have an awful temper. I do and say such stupid things! My husband and children deserve better, but I don't know how to give it to them. I've done such awful things, Lord. I killed my baby. I KILLED MY BABY!!!! Please forgive me! Please, God! I'm so sorry . . . so very, very sorry. I don't know if You want me, but from this point on I give You my life. I give you all that I am and all that I'm not; all that I hate about me. Whatever You want to do with me, I'm willing. Whatever You ask me to do I'll do it. I just can't go on like this anymore. I've made such a mess of everything. Whatever's left of my life is Yours. Change me, please! Forgive me, please!"*

I didn't go forward. I didn't tell anyone. Lightning didn't flash and thunder didn't boom. A beam of light didn't shine down from heaven, but I left the church feeling like a big weight had been removed from me. I felt a small glimmer of . . . hope; something I hadn't allowed myself to feel in a very long time. Though I didn't fully understand it at the time, from that moment on I was changed . . . forever. The hopeless, wounded woman who had walked through those doors less than an hour before no longer existed. An exchange had taken place. Pain, shame and judgment had been exchanged for forgiveness, healing and freedom.

Chapter Seven

To preach good tidings to the poor . . .

In the days following that miraculous event, while thinking about my life and thinking about Jesus, I came to the realization that Jesus loved me anyway. What I had done in my life was exactly why He came to earth – to bring the good news from God that His Son was going to pay the penalty for the sins of humans so that we would not have to. I began to understand God is holy and will not lower His standards of holiness to accommodate our sin – it would have to be punished – but He loves us so much He decided He would send His Son to take the punishment for us so that those who believe Jesus died for them and accept His payment as their own can be forgiven, and having been forgiven can enjoy the close, loving relationship with God He created us to have. And, Jesus loves us so much that He willingly agreed to pay the price for our sin by dying on the cross. I began to experience the inner joy of knowing that God had forgiven me for my abortion, for all my sexual encounters, for every lie I had told, for every drug I had taken, for every person I had hurt and for every single bad thing I had ever done.

I left the church that day feeling relieved and hopeful. It felt good finally telling God what I had done. For years, I had told myself that I was justified in killing my child – that I was too young; that I had the right to kill my child – it was my body; that it wasn't even a child- it was just a little blob of stuff. Yet, for those very same years, deep inside I had known those statements to be a lie and that what I had done was wrong. Finally admitting the same to God and taking responsibility for my actions, instead of making me feel worse about myself as I had previously thought it would, actually made me feel better.

When I got home, I shared the news with my family. I did not particularly feel changed but I knew I felt different. Over the next several months, however, changes occurred that were very noticeable not only to me but to my family. The first change took place almost immediately.

Before I surrendered my life to Christ that day at 38 years of age, I had smoked cigarettes since I was 12 years old. I smoked almost three packs of cigarettes a day and had tried numerous times to quit, all without success. I could never make it past the third day. The Friday before giving my life to Jesus, I had asked my youngest child to throw my remaining cigarettes into the toilet as I was determined yet again to quit smoking. I believed that if I could just make it past the third day, I would be home free. The Sunday I walked into that church they had started a revival so there were going to be church services for the next five evenings. When I returned that same Sunday evening, I asked everyone who spoke to me and everyone I knew there to please pray for God to help me quit smoking. I knew if I could just make it through Monday (the third day of not smoking), I would be through the worst of it and had my best chance of quitting forever. Monday came and I did not smoke. I went to church that evening and again asked people to pray for God to help me quit smoking. Each day came without me smoking and each evening came with me going to church and asking them to pray for God to help me quit. By the time revival was over on that Thursday evening I had gone six days without smoking and I knew I was going to make it. Over the following weeks and months, whenever I would get a craving for a cigarette or be tempted to smoke, I would ask God to help me stay strong. And He did. I was beginning to understand that God was with me and wanted to help me change my life.

The second way I changed that was very noticeable and happened fairly soon was with my mouth. Before that wonderful Sunday morning, I used very foul language, especially when angry, to express myself. My father had a very bad temper and could become violent. Though he never physically abused me, I have many memories of him being rough with my mother and very verbally abusive towards her. When angry at us, he would cuss, scream and break things. When I became an adult, I had a very bad temper myself and when it rose up inside me, I felt I had to get it out or I would explode inside. I could reach a point in anger that I was unable to feel anything but the anger – no pain, no thought of consequences, no compassion. As a mother, I never wanted to abuse my children so I learned that saying cuss words helped dispel the anger. My children grew up learning that the madder I was the worse my cussing became. Though I never struck out at them physically when I was that angry, I still terrified them with my anger, screaming and cussing. The images of their precious faces wide-eyed in terror of me still haunt me to this day. Children should never be afraid of their mothers, but sometimes mine were terrified of me. I would say the worst cuss words in our society in front of them when I was angry, but I also cussed in their presence in my normal everyday talking. I knew it was wrong, but I didn't know how to stop doing it or keep from doing it.

Having grown up with boys and having been around so many men in the years of my youth, I was very crude in my way of speaking. I loved telling the dirtiest, most disgusting jokes. It brought laughs and I thought made people like me.

For a few moments, I had someone's undivided attention and for a few moments I felt important.

Becoming the daughter of the Creator of the universe changed all that. I started noticing when I would cuss and I would not like the way it sounded. I would also feel convicted inside and compelled to tell God I was sorry for saying that. I started noticing the cuss words in shows and movies that I had previously watched without even hearing them. It bothered me to hear those words coming out of someone's mouth. I started paying attention to what I was saying and choosing other words where a cuss word would have previously been said.

The third change took place less than two weeks or so after the revival. I grew up in a drinking family. My mother did not drink very often, but my father and his family often drank to intoxication. Most of my siblings followed suit when they grew up. Though I had done my fair share of getting drunk as a teenager, I did not like the feeling of being out of control, nor the nausea and vomiting that would often occur. As an adult, I realized that almost every bad thing that had happened in my life was related to alcohol in one way or another. I had also learned more about alcoholism and, having seen the effects it had on my family and friends, I tried to pay attention to how much I consumed.

Over the years, I had learned how to drink just enough to maintain the good feeling (or buzz) of the alcohol without losing control. My children actually enjoyed seeing me drink because I became silly, made them laugh and I was much more easy-going. I enjoyed the feeling their approval gave me as I so desperately wanted and needed it. They had no idea how much of a failure I felt as their mother, so I cherished those moments.

One weekend, my husband and I were at the local grocery store and I had picked up a six-pack of our favorite beer. I went over to the produce to pick out some limes when deep inside I had the overwhelmingly certainty that God did not want me to drink anymore. I remembered my promise to Him that whatever He wanted me to do I would do, so I laid the limes down and hurried back to my husband. I explained to Him that I just knew God didn't want me drinking anymore and I was going to put the beer back. I do not think I even made it back to the beer section; I could not get the beer out of my cart fast enough. I no longer had a need or a desire to drink and I learned that I could have just as much fun, if not more, without drinking.

Once Christ helped me lay down the three things I had become dependent upon to handle life, He then got busy dealing with the wounds my childhood traumas and bad choices had caused within my soul . . .

Chapter Eight

To heal the brokenhearted . . .

A child is supposed to be able to trust the adults in his/her life and when that trust is betrayed it wounds the child deeply, in the core of that child's sense of security and self-worth. I had been betrayed by many adults as well as other people throughout my childhood so my security and self-worth were deeply damaged. I felt I always had to earn someone's love –my children's, my husband's, even God's. My heart had been broken so many times by the feeling that I wasn't enough for people; that it was only what I could and did do for people that kept them in my life.

God used my husband to heal one of the biggest wounds in my heart – the wound caused by the betrayal of other men. Even though I had asked God just to bring a man into my life who would be a good father to my children, He went so beyond what I had even asked or imagined! He sent me a kind man who loves my children as his own. A man who has loved me in spite of all the baggage I brought into our relationship. A man who has made it clear that while he loves the physical side of our relationship, he loves the emotional one even better. He likes spending time with me. He encourages me to be all that God wants me to be; in fact, my husband is the one who encouraged me to write this book. He said he believes I have a story that God can use to help a lot of hurting women. He is an honest man and I have learned I can always trust him to tell me the truth. He is a hard-working man with a lot of integrity. He set a good example for our children growing up, showing them the value of being a man of your word, treating people right, doing the right thing and living your life with honor.

Once the church revival ended, I continued to go to church every time the doors were opened. I had a strong sense that I needed to learn as much about Jesus as I could. God had already blessed me by drawing me to a loving, caring church and He made sure to introduce me to many older, godly women who took me under their wings, loved me and taught me. Through these wonderful women and the caring people of my church, Jesus healed the wounds I carried from feelings of rejection and disapproval.

There was one particular lady named Glenda (name changed to protect privacy) whom I had known a few years before ever coming to my church. In fact, she was a big reason I felt comfortable going to this particular church when God was drawing me to Him. We had served together on our children's school's athletic booster program. Glenda often invited me to church and to the various get-togethers and programs they had, but I had always refused. Yet, no matter how many times I declined, she never made me feel judged, she never criticized me or changed her attitude towards me. She just continued being kind and friendly.

After I started attending church, I once told Glenda I enjoyed singing and she encouraged me to come with her to choir practice. She assured me I would love it and they would love having me. The first time I attended choir practice, she introduced me to the choir in general and then specifically to both an older and a younger woman in the section I would be in named Patty and Betty, respectively (again, names changed). These two loving women enveloped me in warmth and welcome. From then on, they both made sure I was sitting/standing beside them. They helped me learn the music and encouraged me to sing out and enjoy worshipping Jesus through song.

Jesus continued to bring women from my church into my life to shower love, affection and praise on me. This was particularly meaningful to me because my Mother had died just shortly before I came to know Jesus and I missed her terribly. She had always been my biggest fan and her love had always soothed the pain of rejection I seemed to carry around with me. These women did and still do mean so much to me. I wish I could name them all for you, but I would much rather Jesus do the honors when they stand before Him. I might mistakenly forget one, but He definitely won't and they each deserve to be remembered.

As I continued to grow stronger in Christ, one of the toughest heartaches for me to overcome was the pain and shame from my abortion. I knew that because of Jesus' sacrifice for me and my acceptance of His payment (His death), God had forgiven me for my abortion, but it took a very long time for me to forgive myself. I still carried around that invisible cloak of shame called "baby killer". I still felt it defined me.

This had been somewhat reinforced, unintentionally perhaps, by the pastor of a church I had attended for a while with my children when they were small. I had overheard one of the ladies in that church talking about how she and others were worried about what some of the teenage girls in the church were involved in. I started thinking that if I could talk to the teenagers and tell them about all the mistakes I had made, including the abortion, perhaps it might prevent them from making the same bad choices. Summoning up all my courage, I went to speak to the pastor and told him about the things that had been done to me and the things I had done, including my deepest, darkest secret – my abortion. Though I cannot remember his exact words, he did not feel that the parents would approve of me talking to their children. I left his office that day feeling not only his disapproval (perhaps only in my own mind), but embarrassed, ashamed and humiliated. I could not bear to face him again so my children and I never returned to that church. Sadly as well, no one from that church ever contacted me afterwards to invite me back or even tell me I was missed, which of course only fueled my belief that I wasn't welcome there.

Many years later, when my husband and I had been attending our new church for only a few months, I believe, I came face to face with my first Sanctity of Human Life Sunday. There on a big screen was an ultrasound film of an unborn baby around the same age as my child when I aborted her. My heart froze in my chest. My breath caught in my throat. Tears of shame, regret and pain welled up in my eyes. I forced them back as I had learned to do for over 20 years. I silenced the screams inside my head and tried my best to act like nothing was wrong. Our youth pastor got up to speak and shared the story of his unborn child that had miscarried. He had held the baby in his hand, noting that it had been fully formed and undoubtedly human. I felt like I was suffocating. Suddenly, I heard the Lord speaking to my heart, *"I want you to tell them about your abortion."* I silently said, *"No, Lord, I can't. Not that. These people like me. If I tell them what I've done, they will hate me."* The Lord brought to my mind the promise I had made to Him, *"Whatever You want me to do, Lord, I will do from this point on."* I leaned over to my husband and told him, *"God wants me to tell them about my abortion. Will it embarrass you?"* He said it wouldn't.

When my pastor stood in the front getting ready to start the time of invitation, I stood up and made my way to the aisle. It seemed I could feel every eye upon me. Fear gripped me like a steel vice, but I knew that I knew that God wanted me to do this. In what seemed like forever, I made it to the front of the church and asked the pastor if I could speak for a moment. With an expression of curiosity and little bit of hesitation, he handed me the microphone and I began to tell my story. I do not remember all that I said, but I do remember being filled with such a love for the teenagers sitting there and a desire for them to know that their choices about sex and drugs can have painful, devastating and lasting consequences that they do not understand at the moment such choices are made.

When I was finished, I felt so relieved that I had been obedient to what Jesus had wanted me to do. Relief soon turned back into fear, however, as I realized that I would have to hand the microphone back to the pastor. As scared as I had been to tell all these people my darkest, most horrible secret, I was even more scared to see the expression I feared would be on my pastor's face. Summoning all the courage and what little pride I had, I turned to the pastor and looked him straight in the eyes . . . . and what I saw there floored me. Instead of disapproval and disgust, I saw compassion and love. Tears were in his eyes and kindness shone from his eyes. God used this loving, caring pastor to start healing my heart of one of my deepest, most damaging and painful wounds. Though I had been obedient to God thinking He was going to use me to bless others, it turns out He had planned all along to bless me and ease an ache in my soul I never thought could be healed.

In the days and weeks following the sharing of my testimony, I received numerous calls and cards from my church family encouraging me and loving me. People came up to me in church and hugged me, telling me how proud they were of me for telling my story. Not one person condemned me. Not one person shunned me. Not one person criticized me. I had never felt such unconditional love from anyone other than my parents. It was a new experience and one that brought unseen changes in my self-perception and filled me with indescribable joy. The tendrils of shame that had started growing when I was but a little child were finally beginning to weaken and lose their grip on me.

Chapter Nine

To proclaim liberty to the captives . . .

According to www.dictionary.com, the word "captive" means "a person who is enslaved or dominated." I once heard Beth Moore describe captives as those who are in [emotional] bondage because of things that have been done to them either as a child or as an adult (such as verbal abuse, emotional abuse, acts of violence such as physical abuse or rape, sexual molestation or sexual abuse, betrayal by a friend or spouse, divorce, abandonment, etc.). Such things can cause us to become captive to a weakened sense of security, a lost sense of self-identity, a damaged sense of self-worth and a warped sense of what love is. We become emotionally "bound" by these thoughts and feelings and they influence how we respond to people, situations and the choices that come our way.

Because of the things done to me as a child, I was held captive by emotional insecurity, very low self-esteem and the false belief that I had to constantly please people in order to keep their affection. Looking back, I can see how many of the choices I made as a teenager were influenced by those mistaken ideas. Thankfully, Jesus was determined to change all that.

Through the preaching and teaching of my pastor, the teachings of Joyce Meyer, Beth Moore and others, the lessons in my Sunday School class and the influence of godly people whom God brought into my life, I began to learn the importance of reading my Bible and spending time with Jesus in prayer on a daily basis. In the pages of that precious Book, I discovered truths about God and myself that changed how I viewed myself and the events of my childhood.

For example, I believed my life wasn't worth much, but the Bible tells me in Psalms 139:13-15:

> *"For you formed my inward parts; you knitted me together in my mother's womb. I praise you, for I am fearfully and wonderfully made. Wonderful are your works; my soul knows it very well. My frame was not hidden from you, when I was being made in secret, intricately woven in the depths of the earth."*

And, in that same Psalm 139 in verses 17 through 18, I learned how often God thinks of me:

> *"How precious also are Your thoughts to me, O God! How great is the sum of them! If I should count them, they would be more in number than the sand; When I awake, I am still with You."*

I believed I was unlovable unless I did something to earn or deserve that love; yet the Bible revealed these truths to me as I read the following Scriptures:

> God has always loved me: *"The LORD appeared to us in the past, saying: 'I have loved you with an everlasting love; I have drawn you with unfailing kindness.'"* (Jeremiah 31:3)

God's love for me isn't dependent upon MY actions: *"But God demonstrates his own love for us in this: While we were still sinners, Christ died for us."* (Romans 5:8)

Over time, these truths began to sink deeper and deeper into my being and be reflected in how I conducted myself. I looked people in the eye. I stopped constantly telling myself I was no good. Words like "ugly," "stupid," "idiot," "failure" and "hopeless" began to disappear from my vocabulary. The chains of self-defeat, self-loathing and low self-esteem that had held me in bondage for so many years began to fall under the love of Jesus Christ and His work in my heart.

Chapter Ten

And the opening of the prison to those who are bound . . .

Prisons are a place of punishment for those who have done wrong; therefore, the prisoners Jesus came to free are those of us who are in bondage due to the choices we have made. Oftentimes, those who are in bondage because of what has been done to them by others (captives) make choices that place them in even deeper bondage (prisoners). Such was the case with me. The low opinion I had of myself and my belief that I had to earn love and affection led me to make choices that only served to make me feel even worse about myself and brought further hardship and struggle into my life.

One such choice, my abortion, caused the death of my own child and almost resulted in my own death through suicide. As I shared with you in a previous chapter, my fear of dying and going to hell kept me from killing myself, and the realization that I could no longer handle my life the way it was drove me to seek God. After confessing all my sins to Christ that day in church, specifically my abortion, and receiving Christ into my life, I understood that God had forgiven me, but forgiving myself for killing my baby was another matter altogether. For several years after receiving Christ into my life, I was still imprisoned by the weight of the shame I felt for having the abortion. On Sanctity of Life Sunday each year at my church, I struggled to hold my head up and not break down in anguished sobs. During those services, I learned more about where my baby was in her development (almost 12 weeks) and my ever-increasing knowledge that she was a human, not a blob of tissue, filled me with such guilt that I found myself doubting that God had truly forgiven me. However, through the preaching and teaching I was receiving, and the times I spent in prayer and reading God's Word, Jesus began to press His truth into my heart. Over time, the following Scriptures helped me to fully accept Christ's forgiveness for my abortion and learn to forgive myself:

Romans 8:1 – *"Therefore, there is now no condemnation for those who are in Christ Jesus . . ."* Christ willingly accepted my punishment, my guilt and my shame for my choice to kill my child. If God Himself has forgiven me, who am I to refuse to forgive myself?

John 8:36 – *"So if the Son sets you free, you will be free indeed."* Refusing to forgive myself for my abortion is like a prisoner having her chains of bondage broken and being told she is free to leave, yet keeping her feet and hands inside the chains and staying in her prison cell.

By accepting the truth of these Scriptures and through the love and support of my husband, children and church family, I was finally able to fully forgive myself for my abortion. This opened the door for Jesus to begin healing the wounds my choice had made to my heart and my soul. He provided opportunities for me to tell others about my abortion and encouraged me to do so. I made it a part of sharing my faith in Christ with those who didn't know Him and I was amazed how often the women He led me to had made similar choices in their lives. The first hint of the thought that God could use me to help other women find forgiveness and healing through Christ for their abortion (and the many other sins I had committed) began to form in my mind.

Around 2009 or so, while attending a Beth Moore conference, I was introduced to the Silent No More campaign.

I spoke with several of the women there who shared their abortion stories with me and how Christ was using them to not only help other women who had had abortions, but to educate people in an effort to prevent abortions from occurring in the first place. I eagerly filled out the contact form expressing an interest in helping others and preventing more babies from suffering the same fate as my child and many, many others.

A short time passed and I received a phone call from the CEO of the SNM organization. During our conversation, she asked me if I had ever participated in a post-abortion Bible Study. I advised her that I had not, though I felt Jesus had already healed me from it. She suggested that I go through one of those studies, which would in turn better equip me for helping other women find healing. Immediately upon hanging up the phone with her, I contacted my local pregnancy support services agency where I was informed that they were starting a new study the following Friday (less than a week away). I sensed God's timing in this and enrolled myself in the study. I met with one of the leaders of the study within a few days and further sensed God's timing and guidance. My relationship with Christ had matured by that time to the point where I knew that I must need more healing that would take place during this study. I had no idea how true that thought would turn out to be . . . .

Chapter Eleven

to comfort all who mourn . . .

The Bible Study *Forgiven and Set Free* by Linda Cochrane was written by a woman who had an abortion for women who have had an abortion, to be offered and taught by women who have had an abortion. Over the 15 weeks of the Bible study (now also offered through weekend retreats), Jesus took me and two other ladies on a journey of accountability, acceptance, forgiveness, acknowledgment, restoration and finally peace; peace with God, peace with ourselves, and peace with our choice. Each of us discovered that though the reasons and circumstances of our abortions were different, the aftermath of insecurity, despair, guilt, shame, self-loathing, depression and self-destructive behaviors and actions were common among us. Our intimate, honest sharing of these things bonded us together in a way that only people who have shared a traumatic experience can bond, yet we had the added benefit of our healing and restoration. The ladies I went through this study with and the ladies who led us through this study are and will always be women I have a deep love and respect for.

The depths of healing Jesus took me to during this study surpassed anything I ever imagined. During this study, Jesus revealed to us the genders and names of our babies, further instilling the needed knowledge that we are their mothers and they are our children. The ladies and I learned through God's Word in the story of the death of David and Bathsheba's baby and other supporting Scriptures that our babies are in heaven, and that if we belong to Jesus Christ by accepting Him as our Lord and Savior, we will one day be reunited with them. This knowledge gave each of us a deep sense of peace and filled our hearts with hope.

But God didn't stop there with me. He took me back into my childhood, teenage years and young adulthood and helped me forgive those who had abused me, betrayed me, used me and abandoned me. He taught me that my unforgiveness wasn't punishing them, it was punishing me. I once heard Joyce Meyer say, "Unforgiveness is like drinking poison hoping the other person will die." Handing them over to God allowed Him to remove that burden from me and freed me to move forward with my life – with my head held high – trusting that He would do right by me.

The revelations Jesus gave me about my childhood, myself, the consequences of my choices, and what His forgiveness really means did more than heal me . . . it set me free. Christ set me free to mourn and then He comforted me. I mourned the loss of my innocence as a child. I mourned the loss of a carefree childhood. I mourned the loss of my virginity that resulted in my loss of a wedding night the way God envisioned me to have. I mourned the lost time with my parents. But most healing and restoring of all . . . . I mourned the death of my child as a mother is entitled to and needs to do. I cried for her. I grieved for her. I ached for her. I named her. As a way of closure on that chapter of my life, I wrote God a letter asking Him to give my baby a message from me and I feel God's leading to share it with you:

Dear Heavenly Father,

Thank You for taking care of my daughter, Tamsyn, for me these past 33 years and healing the wounds I inflicted on her.

Thank You for taking me through this Bible study so that I could be healed from my choice to abort Tamsyn rather than trusting in You to take care of both of us.

Thank You for Your Son, Jesus, through Whom I have received forgiveness and the ability to truly forgive myself and all those surrounding the events leading up to and following my choice to end my baby's life.

Thank You for giving me the capacity to go from denial to accepting the fact that I am a mother who lost a child while at the same time giving me the freedom and ability to love her and grieve for her.

Now, Father, I ask You to please convey the following things to my precious child for me:

1. *Please tell her I am sorry for what I did and all the pain and fear I caused her.*
2. *Please tell her that she has been and always will be a part of me and I will never forget her.*
3. *Please tell her I now understand that my choice to not let her be born in no way diminished her right to the life You had planned for her, nor diminished her worth and value.*
4. *Father, she already knows she is precious to You. Please let her know that she is also precious to me and that I love her.*
5. *Please tell her that I look forward to the day when I can finally hold her in my arms, look into her beautiful eyes, smell her sweet baby smell, and kiss her sweet face as she deserves.*
6. *Please tell her she has two incredible siblings that she will get to meet when You call them home. Please tell her that I am sorry I denied her and them the opportunity to know each other here on earth.*
7. *Please tell her that I love her very much and I miss her.*

8.   *And lastly, Father, please tell her that You and I are not going to let her death be in vain because You are going to use me to speak the truth about abortion – the pain and suffering it causes to both the baby and the mother – and to reach other women who have had abortions and help them realize how much Jesus loves them and how they can find forgiveness and healing at the foot of the Cross.*

The words, "Thank You" are not enough for what You have done for me and inside me. I will forever love You and sing Your praises. And I hereby rededicate the rest of my life and all that I am to You to be used by You as you see fit, all for Your glory and honor.

Because of Jesus, not only were the chains of shame and guilt broken, but He grabbed my hand and helped me step clear of them and walk out of the prison cell I had been in for so many years. I was now free to acknowledge my child, love my child, mourn the death of my child, and share the death of my child with others so that babies like Amber Tamsyn can have a chance at life.

Chapter Twelve

. . . to give them beauty for ashes . . .

Not only did Jesus come to reconcile us to our heavenly Father through the good news to the poor in spirit of His death, burial and resurrection as payment for our sins, give liberty to those held captive by things done to them in their lives and freedom to those held prisoner by the choices they made, He also came to EXCHANGE some things.

Jesus wants to take the ashes of our lives – our mistakes, our sins, our heartaches, our pain, our suffering, our shame – and give us beauty in its place. And He wants to take our regret and sorrow for the things we've done and the mistakes we made and help us do honorable things with them. How does He do this? By instilling in us through His Word the knowledge that He will take what we've done and been through and use it for a greater good, a greater purpose, and make our life and other people's lives better because of it.

Once we give our life to Jesus, everything that once was bad will be used for good. The Bible tells us in Romans 8:28 – *"And we know that in all things God works for the good of those who love him, who have been called according to his purpose."* The individual events may in and of themselves not be good, but once they are under the blood of Jesus through our acceptance of Him in our life, they become His tools for reaching, teaching and changing the lives of others through our testimony.

I am not proud of some of the things I've done and some of the choices I've made, but every time I share my story with others, I often find out that they have made some of the very same choices and mistakes that I have. As I tell them how Jesus has forgiven me and how He has healed and changed me, they begin to see that if Jesus will do that for me, why wouldn't He do that for them. The first buds of hope begin to spring up in their heart. As they begin to understand that Jesus has already willingly taken their punishment for them and only wants them to accept His gift and let Him into their lives, that hope springs to life and His love captures their heart. As I lead them in a prayer that says something like, *"Dear Jesus, I'm sorry for the sins I have committed in my life. Please forgive me. I believe You took the penalty for them in my place so I would not have to. I believe you died on that cross, were buried and rose again. I thank You for shedding Your blood for me. Save me, Jesus. Come into my life and heal me, change me and restore me. You are my Lord and I give You my life and my love. Thank You. Amen,"* I watch as tears of relief, joy and hope fill their eyes and overflow down their cheeks. It is one of the most beautiful things I've ever witnessed. In that moment, the ashes of my life are used to bring beauty into someone else's. In turn, as they begin sharing what Christ has done for them, their ashes become something beautiful. Only God can do something like that!

Chapter Thirteen

. . . the garment of praise for the spirit of despair . . .

Many of us carry around emotional garments (or baggage). Garments of shame, pain, heartache, anger, bitterness or despair that cover our heads and our hearts as we trudge through life. Garments of labels such as "failure", "stupid", "worthless", "liar", "adulterer", "baby killer", "whore", "slut", "no good", "trash", "ugly", "unlovable", "unwanted", "thief", "disappointment", etc. that we believe forever define us and determine our destiny. Garments that weigh us down and keep us from looking ahead with any kind of hope. Garments that prevent us from moving freely in life, holding us back from experiencing the joys that life has to offer.

Jesus came to change all that. He came to remove those burdensome cloaks from our shoulders, those drapes from our heads, and place them all on Him. In exchange, He wants to wrap us in light, freely flowing garments of love, forgiveness, mercy, grace, peace, acceptance and restoration that cover us, yet do not keep us from experiencing life with Him to the fullest – the way He died for us to live. He wants to exchange the labels we drape over ourselves with new labels: "loved", "forgiven", "accepted", "approved", "valuable", "priceless", "beautiful", "strong", "wise", "gentle", "kind". The garments a child of God wears really do define us, and offer us limitless possibilities. As Jesus heals us and we learn to accept who we really are in Christ, an amazing thing happens – we begin to see ourselves as God see us and our hearts become filled with indescribable joy and our lives with unbelievable promise.

For over 30 years, I either would not allow myself to think about my abortion, or I would think of it with such shame and guilt that I thought I would suffocate from it. Accepting God's love and forgiveness, and finally forgiving myself have filled me with such overwhelming gratitude to Him for what He did for me that I can't help but praise Him. I realize that Jesus has taken the most shameful, awful thing I have done and has turned it into a bridge to bring others to the same love, forgiveness and freedom that He has allowed me to experience. He is such an amazingly cool and loving God!

Another garment I carried around for years was bitterness for what was done to me in my childhood and how it affected the course of my life. I came to realize that not only was I bitter towards the people who did that, but I was also bitter at God for allowing it to happen. Why didn't He stop them? Why didn't He protect me from them? Following my surrender to Jesus, I asked God those questions many times. Over the years, He has given me an understanding of things that is somewhat difficult for me to find words to describe in this book, but with His help I'm going to try and I'm praying He will somehow help someone reading this.

Our parents are flawed, sinful human beings just like we are. Some of them are worse than others, some of them are better than others, but they are all flawed. Some do the best they can, some don't even try, but all of them make mistakes. God knew this before He gave us to them. Yet, because each one of us is so unique, so special to God, He had to allow us to be born to our particular parents just so we would exist. You see, God finely crafts each one of us intimately with His own hands and it takes our respective mothers and fathers to provide the material He uses to bring us into being. He uses this gene from our mother to shape our eyebrows, this gene from our father to color our eyes, this gene from our maternal grandfather to give us the sound of our laugh, this gene from our paternal grandmother to fashion our nose, and so on and so on. Psalm 139:13-18 describes this beautifully:

> *"13 For you created my inmost being; you knit me together in my mother's womb. 14 I praise you because I am fearfully and wonderfully made; your works are wonderful, I know that full well. 15 My frame was not hidden from you when I was made in the secret place, when I was woven together in the depths of the earth. 16 Your eyes saw my unformed body; all the days ordained for me were written in your book before one of them came to be. 17 How precious to me are your thoughts, God! How vast is the sum of them! 18 Were I to count them, they would outnumber the grains of sand — when I awake, I am still with you."*

Our Father, God, knows that some of us are going to have horrible childhoods, that some of us are going to be mistreated or abused by our parents or by others as we grow, that some of us are going to be neglected or abandoned, and that some of us are going to have awful, terrible things done to us. It breaks His heart. BUT, it took our parents coming together at that very specific point in time when we were conceived so that each particular gene God had selected would join together in our DNA to create us. You! Me! We are so special and valuable to God that even though He knew some of us would have to go through some bad stuff, it was worth it just to have us in the world.

He also knew that He would be there with us through every moment of it. Though I didn't sense His presence when things were happening to me, I can look back now and see His hand of protection over me. In my case, He protected me from being completely violated by those boys and men. He preserved my virginity through it all (I'm the one who gave it away to the wrong guy). He protected me from getting pregnant at 13 or 14. He protected me from being killed or worse by any of the men I foolishly climbed into vehicles with. He protected me from being <u>violently</u> raped. He protected me from being arrested and going to prison for other activities I got myself involved in.

Some of you may be thinking, "Well, God didn't protect ME from those things." While that may be true, He still was with you every moment. He DID give you the strength you needed to make it through, didn't He? You are here. You survived. And if you will give those memories, that pain, that suffering, that heartache, that sense of betrayal and abandonment, that anger, that bitterness, that hatred to God through His Son, Jesus Christ, God will pour His love and power into each experience, heal them and restore what you lost through them. There is a beautiful promise God gives us in 1 Peter 5:10 – *"And the God of all grace, who called you to His eternal glory in Christ, after you have suffered a little while, will Himself restore you and make you strong, firm and steadfast."* Then, if you will let Him, Jesus will use those very things that caused you such pain to bring hope to others who have suffered or who are suffering through the same thing. When that happens, your pain lessens, your joy increases and your praise intensifies!

Chapter Fourteen

*That they may be called trees of righteousness,
planted by the* LORD, *that He may be glorified."*

The most important thing to God is that people come to Him through His Son, Jesus. He loves each of us so much that He wants us to be with Him forever. We are His greatest desire, His most cherished creation, and everything He does is done with eternity in mind. He knows that our time here on earth is short, but eternity is never-ending, and He works in each of our lives to draw us and others to Him. Our time of life here is like one grain of sand on an ocean beach and eternity is like the grains of sand on every beach, in every ocean, and across every desert. Each of us gets this one grain of time on earth to make the decision about where the rest of our time, our eternal time, is spent and to make an impact on this earth for the kingdom of God.

If we choose Christ as our Lord and Savior, we will spend eternity with God and everyone else who believes in Jesus. If we reject Christ, we will spend eternity separated from God, His love and His peace. God doesn't want that for ANYONE, but they can't come to Him if they don't know about Him. *"But how can they call on Him to save them unless they believe in Him? And how can they believe in Him if they have never heard about Him? And how can they hear about Him unless someone tells them?"* (Romans 10:14) That's where you and I come in.

As Jesus continues to heal me, restore me and mature me, He provides more and more opportunities for me to tell others what He's done for me. I don't have to be a Bible scholar. I don't have to know all the answers. I just have to work with the things I DO know. I KNOW the things I've done. I KNOW how I was feeling before I let Him into my life. I KNOW how He's changed me. I KNOW how He's forgiven me. I KNOW how He's healed me. I KNOW how He's restored me. And I KNOW how He's loved me. That's all I NEED to know. God does the rest. This book is about what God has done in me and for me. It's His story of redemption in my life. As I tell others about what He's done in my life, He is glorified. As I let others see the difference He has made in my life, He is glorified. As I use my story to bring others to Jesus, He is glorified. As I wear the garments and labels Christ has given me, He is glorified. As I continue to let Him guide my life and surrender to His will, He is glorified. I become God's tree of righteousness planted by Him for His glory . . . and the ashes of my life become something beautiful.

It is my prayer that God has spoken to your heart through the words of this book. I pray that something I've said has struck a cord in your life. Sweet one, God longs for you to know Him. Perhaps, like me, you have spent your whole life just wanting to be loved and accepted, to feel like you matter, that you are here for a reason. I pray my story has helped you realize that you are! The love you're looking for is found in Jesus! The acceptance you're looking for is found in Jesus! You were created for a purpose and God has a wonderful plan for your life! It's all to be found at the foot of the cross, underneath the blood of the ONE Person who loves you enough to not only die for you but to take YOUR punishment and bear YOUR suffering so that you wouldn't have to . . . all just so He could be with you. Don't reject His love. Embrace it with open arms. Then, you too will experience a love like you've never known and beauty will come from the ashes of your life.

Ingram Content Group UK Ltd.
Milton Keynes UK
UKHW020959200323
418838UK00012B/1821